THE MOON OF THE
FOX PUPS

THE THIRTEEN MOONS

The Moon of the Owls (JANUARY)

The Moon of the Bears (FEBRUARY)

The Moon of the Salamanders (MARCH)

The Moon of the Chickarees (APRIL)

The Moon of the Monarch Butterflies (MAY)

The Moon of the Fox Pups (JUNE)

The Moon of the Wild Pigs (JULY)

The Moon of the Mountain Lions (AUGUST)

The Moon of the Deer (SEPTEMBER)

The Moon of the Alligators (OCTOBER)

The Moon of the Gray Wolves (NOVEMBER)

The Moon of the Winter Bird (DECEMBER)

The Moon of the Moles (DECEMBER-JANUARY)

NEW EDITION THE THIRTEEN MOONS

THE MOON OF THE
FOX PUPS

BY JEAN CRAIGHEAD GEORGE

ILLUSTRATED BY NORMAN ADAMS

■ HarperCollins*Publishers*

The illustrations in this book were painted with
Winsor & Newton gouache on rag board.

The Moon of the Fox Pups
Text copyright © 1969, 1992 by Jean Craighead George
Illustrations copyright © 1992 by Norman Adams

Typography by Al Cetta
1   2   3   4   5   6   7   8   9   10
NEW EDITION

Library of Congress Cataloging-in-Publication Data
George, Jean Craighead, date
    The thirteen moons : the moon of the fox pups / by Jean
Craighead George ; illustrated by Norman Adams. — New ed.
        p.   cm. — (The Thirteen moons)
    Summary: Describes the experiences of five fox pups during the
month of June in the farmland of Pennsylvania.
    ISBN 0-06-022859-8. — ISBN 0-06-022860-1 (lib. bdg.)
    1. Foxes—Juvenile literature.   2. Foxes—Pennsylvania—
Juvenile literature.   [1. Foxes.]   I. Adams, Norman date, ill.
II. Title. III. Series: George, Jean Craighead, date, Thirteen moons
(HarperCollins)
QL795.F8G38   1992   90-22386
599.74′442—dc20   CIP
                                                          AC

Why is this series called The Thirteen Moons?

Each year there are either thirteen full moons or thirteen new moons. This series of books is named in their honor.

Our culture, which bases its calendar on sun-time, has no names for the thirteen moons. I have named the thirteen lunar months after thirteen North American animals. Primarily night prowlers, these animals, at a particular time of the year in a particular place, do wondrous things. The places are known to you, but the animal moon names are not because I made them up. So that you can place them on our sun calendar, I have identified them with the names of our months. When I ran out of these, I gave the thirteenth moon, the Moon of the Moles, the expandable name December-January.

Fortunately, the animals do not need calendars, for names or no names, sun-time or moon-time, they follow their own inner clocks.

—JEAN CRAIGHEAD GEORGE

ONE AFTER ANOTHER the trees of North America paraded into flower and leaf. The first to color the gray landscapes of the Northeast were the willows. They were followed by the maples, then aspens, wild cherries, tulip trees, elms, dogwoods, sycamores, and beeches. Each tree had its own biological alarm clock that told it when to flower and leaf. The last to bear leaves were the oaks. Their bronze leaflets burst from their buds, unfolded, and turned green. And then it was June.

Bees hummed. Young bluebirds fluttered out of their nests to the excited cries of their parents.

Baby blue jays perched on tree limbs without falling, and crows sneaked through branches to feed their blue-eyed young waiting for them in nests made of sticks. Rain-filled brooks tinkled over the eggs of bass and trout, and the petals of the fruit trees blew away. Dandelions turned silver, cherries ripened; and from dens and hollows, the children of the woods peered out upon a June-green world. The moon of growing up was upon the land.

Among the peekers were five bright-eyed fox pups. It was early evening, about six o'clock. The fox pups were in the entrance of their den at the edge of a woods, staring out at a farm in the Cumberland Valley of Pennsylvania. Across the United States and Canada, from mountain to plain to forest, red foxes live in patches of cover near open spaces where they can hunt mice and small game.

The farm by the Callapasink Creek was a perfect fox habitat. Woods grew along the stream and over the hills. A meadow surrounded a coin-round pond and a vegetable garden. Wooden fences marked off open fields of wheat, corn, and alfalfa.

The fox den was on the wooded hillside above the creek, just far enough back among the trees so as not to be visible to the people, but not so far that the foxes could not keep their eyes on these hunter-neighbors. Last year the fox parents had enlarged and lived in an old woodchuck hole, but this spring they had dug their own den. When it was completed, they called to each other in many high-pitched *wurps* that sounded like human laughter.

On this evening the pups, ears up, black noses wet and shining, were watching and waiting for their parents at the mouth of the den.

A warm wind stirred the whorl of leaves on an Indian cucumber root, a perky wildflower. All the fox pups turned their heads to watch it dance. A June beetle alighted heavily on the flowers of a wild leek plant. All heads turned its way. A yellow star grass dropped a petal. Five pairs of eyes studied it.

A moment later a red-winged blackbird settled on a fragile iris blooming by the creek. The pups cocked their heads and watched the bird. He lost his footing and fluttered down to a yellow mass of swamp buttercups. His mate, who was brooding their newly hatched nestlings in the reeds near the iris, cheeped softly. The pups listened.

A robin flew off the nest she had built of mud and sticks among the white flowers of a wild rose bush. She darted over the fox den. Flying as far as the patch of pale wood sorrel, she dropped a small white object. It was a fecal sac, a little bag of body wastes held in a membrane. She had received it from a nestling. Parent songbirds pick up these bags and carry them far away to keep the nest site clean. The robin circled home, flying low over the blooming whorled loosestrife and the fragrant yellow bells of the spreading dogbane.

The fox pups scanned the distant fields. The farmer was coming home on his tractor. He had been cultivating corn all day.

Suddenly all five pairs of black, fur-trimmed

ears swiveled to the right. A wild geranium had rustled. The leaves of a Christmas fern whispered, and the pups' regal father stepped onto a rock. His red fur shone; his black nose, legs, and tail glistened. His belly fur swung white and soft. The ferns whispered again. The graceful mother stood beside her mate.

The dog fox and the vixen scanned the land for enemies, sensed the rightness of the moment, and signaled to the pups. Theirs was a silent signal—just a twitch of their tails. Having called, they started down the hill. Quietly the pups followed.

For the first time the fox pups ran beyond their play yard, a trampled four- by six-foot area in front of the den. They tumbled over each other in their eagerness to be in the midst of all they had seen—fluttering blackbirds, June beetles, busy robins.

The pups were nine weeks old. One was a male; the other four were females. Their parents had mated in February, and seven and a half weeks later, in early April, the pups were born. They had been well furred on the first day of life.

Their eyes opened ten days later, and they prowled the tunnel. They saw their mother. They stared at her, taking in her shape and face. Finally they saw each other. They whimpered soft greetings.

Although the pups could see, they were still quite helpless. They wobbled when they walked, on legs with bones so delicate they seemed like fragile glass. They still nursed, and they could not clean and groom their fur. They needed their mother constantly, and so their father brought her food. He dropped mice, meadow voles, and rabbits near the den's entrance, for these were the main foods of the foxes, who also eat wild black cherries, a few birds, salamanders, and frogs, in season. Grasshoppers are fox snacks in August and September, as well as apples, blackberries, or an occasional bite of fresh corn.

One day after the pups' eyes opened, the father came partway into the dimly lit tunnel. Fifteen feet back into the hill, the fox pups heard him. They approached him gingerly, sensing his importance.

Having introduced himself, he went away.

As the days passed, the biological clocks inside the pups ticked on, and as they did, they were able to do new things: yip, box, and roll onto their backs. They ate less often. They were awake longer. They were ready to be left alone for several hours, and so the vixen took off to go hunting and to lounge in the sun.

When they were five weeks of age, and stable on their feet, the mother led them up the long tunnel to the entrance of the den. They looked out on the beautiful woodland and farm. Their father lay curled on a nearby rock. He watched cannily for enemies while the pups ventured into the play yard. For hours they smelled plants and rolled pebbles with their paws. When they stumbled with fatigue, the vixen led them back into the den and nursed them.

The next night she began their schooling. She brought a dead mouse to the play yard. At first they stared at it, then sniffed it, and finally the male reached out and touched it. He barked a

high-pitched *weirp*. A sister bit his tail. He turned and bit her tail, then chased his own. Another sister grabbed the mouse. The male knocked her over with his shoulder. She pounced on him, and the mouse was forgotten as the pups boxed and tumbled. The moon of June was moving on, and the clocks of the pups had arrived at "play." They had also arrived at "knowledge." The male pup knew what a mouse was. He had eaten one.

The nights and days revolved. The pups grew on. One evening they were able to scratch behind their ears instead of in the air. A few nights later they reared and pounced in the manner of the fox. With that, their father dragged a dead mouse across the ground and hid it under the leaves. They tracked it down by scent. Just before dawn, lifting their heads into the wind, they picked out the odors of the cattle and the people on the air. Their clocks had ticked to "smell."

Now they were ready to follow the dog fox and vixen into the woods and fields. And so this evening, after watching the blackbird, the beetle, and the robin, they ran out of their play yard and followed their parents into the bigger world.

At the bottom of the hill their father, the dog fox, halted. The vixen stopped in her tracks; but the pups, who were not yet coordinated, bumped into their parents' tails and each other before finally braking to a stop. Their father was pointing with his nose to something on the ground. A box turtle, head and legs inside her bony carapace, was settled on the earth. Her shell was closed. The dog fox picked her up and placed the stone-like reptile among his pups. The pups cocked their ears and sniffed her. This was no mouse. The turtle opened her "door" slightly. A pup nosed her, and the door shut on the little wet nose. The pup yelped in pain. The other pups drew back in respect. Satisfied that his offspring knew a box turtle, the dog fox turned and trotted toward the stream. The family followed stealthily.

The turtle, using the earth as a sounding board, waited until the vibrations from the fox steps died

away. Then she opened her shell, thrust out her feet and hard, blunt head, and walked. She went back to the spot where the fox had picked her up and began to dig with strong, slow thrusts of her hind feet and claws. She made a hole about four inches deep. In this she laid six leathery eggs, then pushed the loam back over them. In the earth nest the eggs would slowly develop, until, on some cool night about October first, the little turtles would break out of their shells and struggle up to the woodland floor.

The eggs laid, the turtle thumped away, not remembering the day in May when she had been the object of a fierce and noisy turtle battle. On that day a male had found her eating wild-lily bulbs. He tapped her shell with his bony chest plate and invited her to be his mate. At that moment another turtle came around a stone and lumbered toward the pair. He desired the female, too. The first male struck his rival with his nose. He struck again, and then, with resounding blows, thumped him with his chest and head until his own nose was bleeding. Finally he turned the rival onto his back in ignominious turtle defeat. Then he knocked on the female's shell once more, and she accepted him. Now, at twilight in the month of June, she had laid her eggs and left them for the earth to incubate.

The swift-footed foxes followed the stream shore to the meadow. The dog fox paused and crouched. A fat young woodchuck was eating grass beneath a sycamore tree. He had been born on the same day as the fox pups, but he had developed faster than they. When he was only four weeks old, he came out of the den to eat clover and grass. Two weeks later when his mother's milk dried up, she drove him and his two sisters from the burrow. She was done with rearing them. They were on their own.

The young chuck had walked away from his mother, but then turned back. She threatened him again, and this time he ran. He sped among silver dandelion heads to the flowering meadow, far from his mother. Here he dug himself a burrow and lived in peace until this moment.

Now he was frightened—the dog fox was stalking him. The young woodchuck was about to scurry down his burrow when the fox stood up, lifted his head, and walked away.

The woodchuck went back to his meal of clover, unaware that the dog fox and the vixen were scheming against him. She was crouched in the weeds, just out of his sight. Suddenly, with a dancer's grace, she leaped out of the grass and took him in her mouth. One shake and he was senseless, but by no means dead. The vixen carried him to her pups to show them this fox food.

The young male picked him up and lifted him high. A sister snatched him away, and he charged her. Regaining his senses, the chuck rolled swiftly to his four short legs, stood up, and growling, slashed out with his sharp rodent teeth. Five surprised pups learned the fury of the woodchuck before he dashed into his burrow.

The parents did not chase the chuck, for there

were other lessons to be taught. The dog fox switched his tail and led his family into the orchard.

Under an apple tree he paused and glanced up into the branches. The orange breast of a male northern oriole glowed among the small green apples as the bird threw back his head and sang his beautiful song to the evening. The dog fox passed right on by him to say that the oriole was not food.

In an elm tree nearby the mother oriole was incubating eggs in a soft gray basket she had made from fibers stripped from thready milkweed and grapevine stems. The nest had taken her six days to build. On the first day she had made a circle of threads in a fork of the tree. Next she began to weave, flying around and around the circle, pushing fibers in and out until she had an open-toed "sock." She wiggled inside the sock and closed the toe with her weavings. As she worked, she chirped to herself.

Occasionally her mate brought her threads for

the nest, but for the most part, he just sang. By the time of the crescent moon of June, the female had finished her nest and laid her full clutch of eggs, one each morning for five days. Then she incubated them. The male stayed nearby as if to encourage her in her lonely task. The fox pups did not see the nest high above their heads on the drooping tip of a limb.

They came to a puddle in the lane. With a burst of white wings, a hundred cabbage butterflies flew up into the air. The fox pups *wurp*ed and chased them among the daisies. The vixen circled the bouncing pups and rounded them up like naughty sheep. They were too frolicsome. The goshawk would see them and attack. Herding them to their father, she snarled until they crouched in silence. One by one the butterflies dropped back to the puddle. A few, however, flitted off to the garden. In the moist evening air they alighted on the cabbages and searched for sheltered spots to lay their eggs.

The fox family arrived at the edge of the creek.

The pups had never been so close to rushing water, and they stared at it curiously. Boldly, the young male stuck in his nose and sniffed. He yelped in pain, sneezed, and pawed his face. Sitting down, he looked at his father for an explanation. The dog fox trotted to the creek edge and lapped. The young male lapped, too.

A catbird in the willows heard the fox pup yelp. With a cry, he flew to a twig in full view of the family, vibrated his wings, flicked his long gray tail, and hopped a little higher. He was distracting their attention from his mate and five fat youngsters, who were cuddled in a nest of sticks in the greenbrier patch.

The little birds were five days old, and like the pups, they were growing up. Just this morning they had attempted to preen their feathers for the first time. They had also yawned. Until this day they could do very little—just lie on their bellies, open their mouths, and defecate in little sacs like the robins. Tomorrow, according to their inner clocks, they would stand for the first time. On the seventh day they would lift their wings up and spread them to the side. On the tenth day they would shake themselves. On the eleventh day they would leave the nest and sit on twigs in the brier patch.

Here they would hop, jump, flutter, and walk up stalks. They would make short flights. On the twelfth day they would sleep with their bills in their back feathers, and on the thirteenth day they would be able to pick up food in their beaks, wag their tails, and drink. A day later they would have developed so far, they would be able to give the the alarm call of the catbird. On and on they would grow in bird skills, until by September they would be as independent as their parents. In October they would fly south to Florida and the shores of the Gulf of Mexico for the winter. It takes a long time to grow.

The five pups watched the scolding, flapping catbird just as he wanted them to do, and so they did not see his nest in the greenbrier patch, nor would they have been interested if they had.

Foxes prefer mice to songbirds, although they would take a bird if it fell before them. Mice are easier to catch.

The dog fox called his family and they trotted along the creek shore. Still not master of his feet, the male pup made an unpardonable fox error. He snapped a stick. The sound frightened a mallard duck who had brought her brood under the drooping willow limbs to spend the night. She squawked, and streaked out across the surface of the water. Fifteen downy ducklings followed, a huge family. The mother had incubated not only her own ten eggs, but five more. A young female, confused by the excitement of the May egg-laying time, had deposited her eggs in the wrong nest. This did not matter to the older mother. She simply incubated and hatched them all. Now she was herding them all across the creek, far from the duck-eating foxes.

When darkness came, the dog fox led his family to the farmhouse. They smelled the barn swallows under the eaves of the porch. The young birds had been flying over and around the farm catching insects all day. Before dusk they had come home to roost for the night, even though their mother was incubating a second clutch of eggs. They settled down in the eaves not far from her. She did not chase them away as the mother woodchuck had done, for the barn swallows are cooperative birds. The first babies help to feed the second round of hungry mouths.

The moon came up. It lit the flowering heads of the wheat and the foot-high blades of corn. The fox pups followed their parents past the fields and along the side of the barn where a day-old calf lay with its mother. They stumbled from weariness. Quick to sense their needs, the vixen led them back to the den, leaving her mate to hunt food for them all.

The next evening the pups were full of energy. They rolled and tumbled in the play yard while they waited for their parents to take them out again. A bullfrog croaked from the edge of the farm pond, then another croaked, and another.

June is the breeding season for these, the latest frogs of the Northeast to sing and lay their eggs. They sounded like mournful bassoons.

Presently the father fox came up the hill and led the pups to the pond. The vixen ran beside him. At the water's edge he skirted grass and reeds until he found a delicious bullfrog. Rearing to his hind legs, he leaped, missed, and frightened the amphibian. It dove into the water with a splash, to the excitement of the little foxes. They ran around the pond scaring the big frogs and learning their habits.

As many skills as the puppies now had, they still had to learn the more subtle sounds of the woods and field. One night by the creek they saw their father twist his ears to say he had heard a noise. They listened, but the marsh was quiet. A furry nose appeared in a hole not two feet from them. A young muskrat rushed out of his den, gnashing his teeth as his mother chased him. The moon of growing up had cast its spell. Like the wood-chuck's mother, his mother was making it quite

clear that it was time for her offspring to go seek his fortune.

The young muskrat did not look back at her. He closed his nostrils and dove into the water. So upset was he that he did not even see the foxes watching him. He swam until he reached the other shore, then pulled up on the embankment and rested. Nearby, another homeless juvenile was eating cattail fruits. They set out together to explore the creek; and by the night's end, both had forgotten their mothers and were digging homes of their own.

As the moon was beginning to wane, the fox pups were chewing old bones, sticks, stones, acorns. Their baby teeth were falling out, their sharp adult ones coming in. They chewed whatever they found. One evening when the male pup bit his father too hard while playing, the dog fox got to his feet and swished his tail. It was time for the pups to hunt, not just look.

The dog fox and the vixen began the hunting lessons by chasing mice to the pups, or scaring a rabbit their way. After many misses the pups were finally successful, and their growls became deeper and more serious.

One night the young male fox came upon the warm trail of a meadow vole. Legs flying, nose in the wind, he raced along its scent. A mother pheasant, incubating her eight olive-brown eggs, listened in alarm as he came toward her. She pressed herself tightly against her eggs and sat perfectly still, as if frozen. The pup did not see the pheasant. He ran right past her, and caught the vole at the bottom of a fence post.

The next night was hot. The foxes stayed within the coolness of the earth, but the insects crept and flew. Their season of greatest activity was just beginning. In the grasses young crickets crawled. They had recently hatched from eggs in the soil, and although they looked much like their parents, with their long antennae and big heads, they were still growing up.

The young crickets could not sing. It would be August before they would fill the day and night

with chirps. Occasionally, however, one tried. A young cricket lifted its stubby wings. The musical instrument of the cricket is a file on the edge of one wing, which is rubbed against a saw on the other. This makes only a small sound, so within the wing of every cricket is an amplifier, a megaphone-shaped box, that enlarges the minute scraping noise into a blast.

The young male fox saw the young cricket near the den door and came out to see what it was. He nosed him. The cricket scurried under a leaf. The pup did not pursue him, for a new scent was on the wind. He didn't know what the scent was, but it made his mouth water. He traced it to the bottom of the hill. There he learned that strawberries are delicious.

As the fox pups learned to hunt, their mother's milk diminished, and she, like the woodchuck and muskrat, became quite irritable when her offspring begged for milk. One night she snapped at the male fox pup. He backed away, turned, and ran down the hill. He had never left his family group before; but tonight was different. He felt comfortable on his own.

He trotted to the stream. He was not as round and fat as he had been when the quarter moon had risen. His legs were longer, and he did not tumble when he walked. He was a graceful juvenile fox.

Beneath an oak he stopped. Something had sailed through the limbs. It sailed back. His sharp eyes picked out the shape of a small flying squirrel among the leaves. Gray, with a flattened tail and large eyes, and trimmed with velvet black, the pretty animal saw the fox, gathered his feet under him, and leaped. He spread his front and hind legs. Membranes covered with fur made "sails" between his wrists and ankles, and he soared off into the night. A limb was in his way. The young squirrel reefed in his right sail and swerved around the limb, lost altitude, and alighted at the bottom of a maple. He ran to the top of the tree and sailed off again.

Born in an old woodpecker hole at the end of March, the flying squirrel had come into the

world feeble and naked. His eyes had not opened for twenty-eight days. A week later he had been weaned, and in another week, like the fox pups, he had followed his mother into the woods. He had an inner clock, too, and when he was eight weeks old he made his first short glide. Now an expert at this mode of travel, he flew off through the woods to hunt seeds and nuts.

The juvenile fox leaped silently over a log and glided up the creek shore. On a sycamore trunk he came upon two big cecropia moths quivering their wings. They are the largest of the North American moths. The male had followed a scent of the female for three miles before finding her. In a few days she would lay her eggs and die. The life of a moth is not long.

The juvenile looked curiously at the beautiful moths and walked on. They were not fox food. He came to the creek and, stepping into the water, walked in deeper and deeper until he was swimming. He circled a pool, then came ashore. Shaking off the water, he pulled a wet leaf from

his chest and licked his legs and feet dry. He was at last old enough to clean and groom his fur.

The moon of June had waxed and waned. Its dark side faced the earth. Twenty-seven and a third days had passed since the June moon had appeared in the sky. Although the night was dark, the juvenile fox saw well with his yellow, light-gathering eyes. He saw the bats escort their young out of the farmhouse attic and over the pond to catch insects. He saw the newly hatched fish in the shallows spread out across the bottom to sleep. In the trees he saw the male fireflies glow as they called to the females in the grass. All these sights lured the young fox to continue.

From now on he would see his family less and less until finally, in autumn, he would take off in a straight line across the country. He would travel perhaps a hundred miles to find a patch of cover near open spaces where he would live out his life.

The young fox trotted along the creek shore, around the pond, and off across the meadow. He investigated the fields on the next farm. The moon of growing up was done.

Bibliography

Burt, William H., and Richard P. Grossenheider. *A Field Guide to the Mammals*. Boston: Houghton Mifflin Company, 1976.

Carter, Anne. *Ruff Leaves Home*. New York: Crown Publishers, 1986.

Hartley, Deborah. *Up North in Winter*. New York: E.P. Dutton, 1986.

Kjelgaard, Jim. *Haunt Fox*. New York: Holiday House, 1954.

Lavine, Sigmund A. *Wonders of Foxes*. New York: Dodd, Mead, 1986.

Leighner, Alice Mills. *Reynard*. New York: Atheneum, 1986.

McDearmon, Kay. *Foxes*. New York: Dodd, Mead. 1981.

MacQuitty, Miranda. *Discovering Foxes*. New York: Bookwright Press, 1988.

Palmer, Ralph S. *The Mammal Guide*. Garden City, NY: Doubleday & Company, 1954.

Schneiper, Claudia. *On the Trail of the Fox*. Minneapolis, Minn.: Carolrhoda Books Inc., 1986.

The World Book Encyclopedia. Vol. 7, p. 379. Chicago: World Book Inc., 1983.

Index